INCREDIBLE COUNTRIES

INCREDIBLE COUNTRIES

A gathering of poems

COLIN OLIVER

Cover design by Sam Blight

Published by The Shollond Trust
87B Cazenove Road
London N16 6BB
England

headexchange@gn.apc.org
www.headless.org
The Shollond Trust is a UK charity, reg. no 1059551

Copyright © Colin Oliver 2017
Design and conversion to ebook by rangsgraphics.com

ISBN 978-1-908774-27-9

for Catherine Harding

with love

Preface

My intention in making this selection of poems is to represent the range of my work from 1970 to the present. It includes poems from *In The Open* (Shollond Publications, 1974), *Seeing* (Interim Press, 1980), *Ploughing At Nightfall* (Downstream Press, 1993), *Stepping Into Brilliant Air* (Head Exchange Press, 1996), *High River* (Downstream Press, 2006), *Saying Goodnight* (Downstream Press, 2011), *Nothing But This Moment,* an e-book of selected poems (Shollond Trust, 2013) and *The Roundness Of Joy* (Downstream Press, 2016).

Grateful acknowledgements are due to the above publishers and to friends and family who have encouraged and supported me over the years. Malcolm Ryan's illustrations for High River I find particularly sensitive and evocative.

I would like to give special thanks here to Richard Lang of The Shollond Trust—who inspired this book—and to Mary Blight of Rangs Graphics, Western Australia.

The poems are arranged in roughly chronological order. Many early ones are expressive of seeing into that transparent inner nature which I believe we all share but so often overlook. Later poems widen the scope but are suffused, I think, with the same essential awareness. I have carried some home from the fields and hedgerows intent on keeping observations spare and scrupulous. Occasionally the subject of renewal in different guises has pressed itself upon me, like a refrain. Here are also bitter-sweet memories involving experiences and people called into the present and held with a tenderness.

It is my hope that the reader will discover poems in this book which will be like stepping stones to a place of stillness.

Colin Oliver

CONTENTS

Preface	vii
Bees	1
Wolf	2
Evening	3
Cold Mountain	4
At The Bridge	6
Haiku	7
Thought-Bees	8
Sea Shell	9
Late Afternoon	10
Visiting Friends	11
Peeling Potatoes	12
Peace	13
The Oneness Of Things	14
Marriage	15
Light	16
Boundless	17
Birthday	18
Hedgebank	19
Storm	20
The Last Spark	21
Windswept	22
Heatwave	23
Fogbow	24

Estuary	25
Beach	26
The Pond	27
Haiku	29
After Rain	30
The Chapel	31
Ploughing At Nightfall	32
The Boy In The Glade	33
A Flicker Of Green	34
River	35
Moon Stories	36
Trees	38
Scents	39
In The Vast Sweep Of Heaven	40
Snowfall	41
High River	42
Haiku	43
Field And Sky	44
Equinox	45
Morning Walk	46
Bumble Bee	47
Sunday	48
Summer Rain	49
Lullaby	50
Shady Trees	51
Night Storm	52

This Hour	53
Wind Chill	54
Wood Mouse	55
Midwinter Sun	56
Haiku	57
A Child Melts Into His Day	58
A Skip Down The Lane	59
The Nag's Head	60
George	61
I Find You	62
With Olly And Isaac In August	63
Jewel	64
Dragonflies	65
Kindling	66
Fetching The Boy	67
Blue	68
Days Later	69
To Tip A Word	70
Chestnut Loke	71
Sparrowhawk	72
Migrating Frogs	73
The Kiss	74
A Root Of Mint	75
Only The Names	76
To Douglas	77
I Walk Into The Weather	78

Caedmon	79
If I Could	80
Saying Goodnight	81
Haiku	82
Foxes	83
Haymaking	84
Teasels	85
I Wake As Crystal	86
The Early World	87
About the writer	89

POEMS

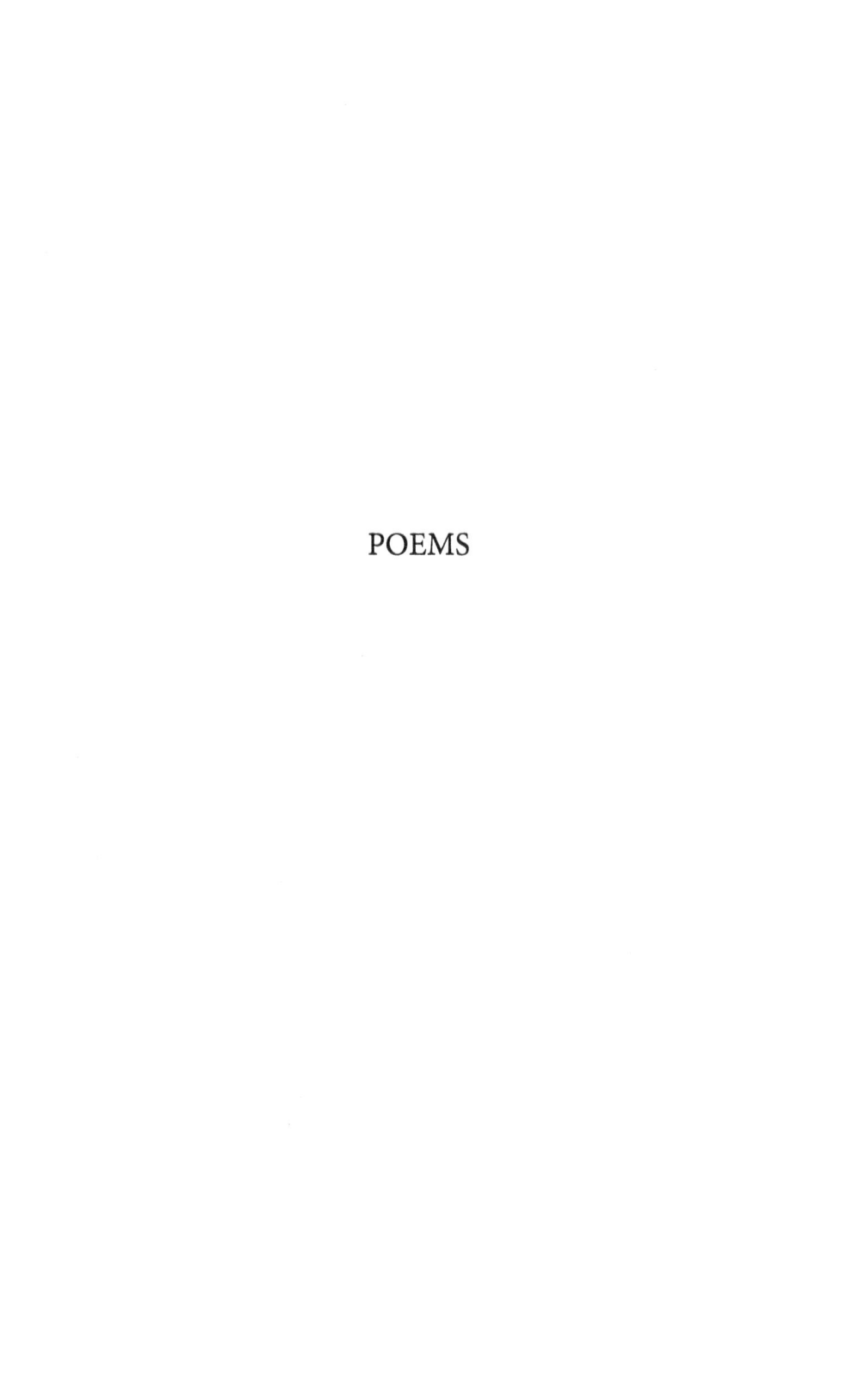

Bees

    To the orchard

    we take the new hive

    and put on our veiled hats.

    The swarm hangs

    among the apple blossom.

    Down they drop

    with one shake

    of the branch -

    half a bucket of bees!

    Poured into the hive

    they quieten

    to the drip of syrup.

    Watching,

    I'm a veiled hat

    with nobody inside.

Wolf

World I am you;

I cannot be kept at bay.

A wolf, I take all

in one bite.

My features have become

nothing but mouth,

a mouth nothing but air.

Here on the plain

of openness

I am ever new to myself.

And the world before me

is like a forest

on which suddenly

snow has fallen.

Evening

> Stopped on the path to listen
>
> to a warbler in the reeds,
>
> between myself and these
>
> reeds, stones, dry cracks in the earth,
>
> there is no distance:
>
> I have become seeing.
>
> Overhead a plane circles,
>
> lights winking, and goes.

Cold Mountain

(After Han Shan)

1

When I came to Cold Mountain

I made my home among pines

at the foot of a green cliff.

Yet who is here? Cold Mountain:

a vacant house. Jagged peaks,

white clouds and crying monkeys.

2

After a shower rocks gleam

and Cold Mountain from high peak

down to green border shimmers.

I wander by a clear stream,

watch pebbles in the water,

slip about on the wet moss.

3

In a valley where mist hangs

I sit by a rock, stay clear,

and see no inside or out.

At sunset, arriving home,

I stretch and take off my cap,

find it beaded with moisture.

4

I fetch water from the pool

where the herons fish; I share

the mountain fruit with monkeys.

At the centre I have found

a jewel and gained nothing.

The wind hums in the pine trees.

At The Bridge

On the way home I stop

at the bridge, the river

rising as the snow thaws.

I am transparent: here

only water, and on

the castle mound the stone

wall like an animal

peering across white fields.

Haiku

every flower in
his first flower-smelling year
is a daffodil

in honeysuckle
over the blackbird's nest
the mother's eye

here I see no-one
to cast on the petals of
this rose this shadow

the delight I feel
goes stamping up the road in
the little boy's coat

on this road
only my torchlight moves
this winter night

Thought-Bees

If thoughts were bees,
who would dare to shut them
tight in the hive of the head?

He who shatters
this hive of pretence
with the swift hammer of seeing,

sees no box, no house,
no door to lock.
The spell of images is broken

and the swarm
breaks out
to scatter in the world.

The hive of nothingness
brings to the world
the honey of love,

and thought-bees,
watched by the queen
of the eye, roam free.

Sea Shell

What secret lies
in the heart of a sea shell
you cannot tell.

But if one day
a shell on a rock should crack
and break its back

your gaze may fall
to find in its secret heart
nothing at all.

Then turning round
to the sea you may wonder
that the waves' sound

can come from an empty heart.

Late Afternoon

    Late afternoon, the rain passed, I go out

    to post a letter. Leaves on the chestnut

    lift in the wind. Nothing but this moment:

    my hand lifts, the mouth of the box drips rain.

Visiting Friends

    A hedge wild with hawthorn,

    bramble, dog rose,

    dogwood, wild hop and old man's beard.

    We walked down to see it

    and share now both view

    and the eye that sees.

    The river is dry,

    rugged with hoof marks.

    Flints in the bank were once heated

    to drop in water skins.

    Feather in hand, my son

    stumbles after

    a chicken that will not keep still.

Peeling Potatoes

    This morning, after rain

    had cleared the air, sparrows

    ranged over the cornfield.

    I stood at the window

    in the kitchen where now

    I peel these potatoes.

    They come white from the knife,

    roll into the water.

    I am clear and look down

    as if from a window.

Peace

    is the station

    where one waits

    but with nowhere to go

    and where

    the grain

    of a bench runs

    like rails through

    incredible countries.

The Oneness Of Things

> The sun low over the beach:
>
> shining wires of dune grass,
>
> stones and the shadows of stones.
>
> On the shoreline, the rush of foam
>
> mirrored in the wet sand.
>
> In the oneness of things
>
> I am nowhere in sight.

Marriage

(for Carole)

To see your face

with the eye of emptiness

is to have your face

as my own, and to find

between seeing and loving

not even a hairbreadth.

Light

> The interior light
>
> is nothing but light;
>
> light upon light.
>
> It is a still pool.
>
> Fingers that try to touch
>
> will, without a ripple, disappear.
>
> The interior light
>
> is the clear light of being.
>
> The light on the rock.
>
> Close to, the eye
>
> may catch the swing
>
> of the lamp of amazement,
>
> but the light itself
>
> is nothing but light;
>
> light upon light.

Boundless

> Like the wind searching,
>
> lifting feathers round
>
> the sparrow's neck,
>
> lifting leaves in a wave
>
> across the bean field,
>
> I find no place
>
> where I can say,
>
> here my being ends.

Birthday

> The gale dying, cypresses on the bank
> rock with the last gusts.
>
> A bale hangs in the hedge,
> water shudders along a wheel track.
>
> My fingers hook into the rough bark
> of logs I stack by the house.
>
> My being is too airy to define
> the particular feel of thirty years.
>
> I stretch and listen to jackdaws
> chacking in the cold March air.

Hedgebank

Hollowed out, I am drawn

to these embers,

smoke dwindling to a wisp.

Rabbit bones bleach in the grass.

I lift the pelvis

over the seedhead it rings.

Sky is a tilted mirror.

I am unshielded,

the hedgebank drones inside me.

The crick of grasshopper,

the fieriness

as thistles burst and blow.

Storm

The storm hangs a veil to the sea.

I bolt down the shingle, stones running.

A downpour drenching in seconds,

a great bulb flashing on the saltmarsh.

Ruts in the cart track brim and stream,

a toad crawls from the flood into grass.

The air cracks, yards off, and I reel,

shocked outwards, becoming all I see.

The Last Spark

>Poppies burn out
>
>at the brink where I stand
>
>blossoms in the chestnut
>
>gutter and shadows
>
>dowse the lights in the river
>
>under the skirt
>
>of boughs the dark
>
>hole of the water rat looms
>
>and I am the slate
>
>wiped clean the nothingness
>
>that sees the last spark die
>
>on the wing of the swift.

Windswept

No shelter for my windswept face.

The shaking seeds

of the lime are wrapped in leaves.

The streetlight is ringed with filigree.

But I am lost, like the hill

darkened to sky,

irresistibly oned with night.

Heatwave

    Past the stone
    where the lizard plays dead
    I see myself gone

    nettles puff seeds like smoke
    the snake slips into reeds

    and the elder
    in the hedge runs
    wild with berries.

Fogbow

Droplets cling to thorns

in grey stillness

threads link tall grasses.

I hold now

what held me small

this squabble in the heart.

As sunlight

breaks I am utterly seized -

the fogbow straddles the high field

and with strange

grace I am pitched

into air.

Estuary

    In biting wind a whirr

    of rigging I turn my back

    hunched coat collar high

    winter trees grip the cliff

    lean over sand and debris

    thin shine of grass

    topknots of mooring posts

    cold dull thud of oars

    dropped in a rowboat

    and I see then the mud

    gleam tide rising and look

    back suddenly faceless

    widening in a breath

    out to estuary spaciousness

    where clouds in their cold

    glory funnel with the sun

    into the west.

Beach

Wind scoured field, low tree stiffened in a lurch,

bramble pared down, its thorns bare and pale.

I drag my heels, fearing disappearance.

Down through dunes, the dune grass quivering.

Stinging sand, wave spray. How like undressing,

this slow shedding of appearances.

With one certainty, my clearness like glass,

I stand in the gleam of stones and sea.

The Pond

The morning light replaces me

with blunted grass, the pinprick glint of frost.

A crackle underfoot, a stone

wrenched up and lobbed, skitters on ice.

*

Fog condensed in the trees to a glimmer

rains on the water.

As I stand under blackthorn, the blossom

reaches out of nothingness.

*

A blackbird's pick-pick warning as I move,

a transparency fringed with reeds.

On the pond a nervous crimple of wind,

in the sky a sliver of moon.

*

Where hedges white with elder wave,

I find no stop to myself.

Leaves pick light from the water,

pitch-black rooks step into brilliant air.

Haiku

foghorn morning
cormorants dive apart
rise together

wind across the pond
frogspawn
riding the wrinkles

on the lowest branch
the sparrow shrieks
at the sleeping cat

puffing up dust
as it follows a toad
the dog's nose

night black rain black
lapwings
piping in the field

After Rain

        After rain, a pure light defines

        what we are:

        the glass edge on leaves,

        the dash of swallows, knee high

        through the field,

        or clouds at the brow of the hill

        backing off for miles.

The Chapel

    The peninsular road peters out

    at the chapel, stone built, shaped like a barn.

    Past the dead stillness of elms,

    the beetle flexing at shadows.

    Inside, sparrows in the rafters,

    dust motes in slants from high windows.

    We bring nothing here.

    What is received is a tidal roar to the ear.

    Later, on saltmarsh paths through grass

    and sea lavender, we are overshadowed still.

Ploughing At Nightfall

> The hill lights burn like a fuse.
>
> The magpie flies the hedgerow
>
> white, white, white.
>
> The tractor roars down its beam,
>
> the plough glowing.
>
> And, pressing on the small door of the self,
>
> the night's immense emptiness
>
> comes falling in.

The Boy In The Glade

    The fat leaves buckle as he passes
        and brush him with their soft leathers.
    The oak and the ash are poised.
    Their heads are filled with intricacies.
    Not one footfall cracks and explodes
        into wings and cries.
    His breathing is the smallest wafting of air
        and a deer stands close and watches,
        its ear ticking in a shaft of light.
    When he kneels at the pool the moss sighs.
    His cupped hands break the water
        like a ghost melting into a mirror.
    He drinks and the coolness threads inside him.
    He bathes his face in transparency
        and he pours it over head and neck.
    The water splashes back into rings.
    And the rings run to the bank
        with little strands of light,
        and whisper to the roots.

A Flicker Of Green

The wild man perched on a high bluff.

His hand reached to a cloud

and his fingers entered the flow.

A white swirl clasped his wrist.

Then his arm in a shiver lifted its hair,

a momentary vision,

like a field of running grass.

The wind scrambled the cliff,

rounded the rocks and stopped in its tracks.

Its howl died to a moan,

the moan to a breath.

A dustcloud sifted to a whisper in the dunes.

Spindrift prickled the dry beach.

Mirrors in the seafoam

closed their lids with a snap.

And the sleeping world, turning in its rags,

dreamed a flicker of green.

River

    The sunlit river was a mirror.
    The wild man's tears fell
    from the sky down to the sky.

    Teardrops flashed into dragonflies
    skitting to the tips of reeds.

    Teardrops inflated to frogs
    kicking into widening circles.

    Teardrops stretched into minnows
    nibbling at the stems of weeds.

    Teardrops roiled the mud,
    rising as little fists of water-lily
    to open their palms.

    Teardrops spotted a pad,
    rushing from splayed feet
    into startled moorhen.

    She stepped away, with a flick
    of her tail, and was gone.

Moon Stories

1

The wolf, the moon heavy in her belly,

padded on pine needles.

On a ridge, in darkness, she retched.

With a surge the moon grazed her fangs

and rolled into the sky.

Quivering, bereft, she howled in its wake.

2

The whale sleeping on the wide sea

woke to the moon

running in silver to her eye.

Her mouth gaped and she gulped

a booming seafall.

The sea drained down, streaking the beaches.

Starfish squirmed, anemones

drew in their tentacles.

3

The owl in the wood was blinded by moonlight.

Her neck ruffled and she hooted,

casting darkness from her beak.

It fell in silence through the branches,

settling under leaves and the ears of fungus.

Under the ferns of the wood,

like black snow, the shadows fell.

4

The wild man meandered through the night.

Roots and slender trunks with leafy twigs

threaded from his mouth.

He dug with his hands and tenderly

planted the saplings,

tamping the soil at their roots.

He moved over the brown earth,

stepping lightly, speaking trees.

Trees

The hazel stood in a bush,

cobnuts in their frilly skirts

curtsying to the breeze.

The hawthorn hid under froth,

a white bouquet,

like milk poured from a pail.

The alder perched by the river

with scaly feet clutching,

ruffling its leafy hearts.

The sallow had springy branches

like young goats chased by bees,

tails waving goodbye.

Scents

The child tilted its head to the breast,
nose gliding on the scent.

The hay lifted the child high,
as on horseback, above meadows of sweetness.

Honeysuckle gently gripped the nape
and pulled the head down to fragrance.

The bucket's pock as it hit the well water
sounded the depth of damp leaf air.

Mushrooms in an earthy stir
opened the little springs in the hollow of the mouth.

Lavender wafted a dreamy stream
fluttering in the nostrils and closing the eyes.

In The Vast Sweep Of Heaven

    Inside the person the secret

        and inside the secret,

        curled north to south, the country.

    Inside the country the lair

        and inside the lair,

        curled head to tail, the wolf.

    Inside the wolf the womb

        and inside the womb,

        curled nose to knee, the child.

    Inside the child the heart

        and inside the heart,

        curled east to west, the stars

        in the vast sweep of heaven.

Snowfall

All night

the white flakes

swirl from the back of blackness.

The fields enter the silence

of a holy order.

A world in silk

where the morning sun

comes teetering

and doves rise

from an apple tree bough,

wings milking the light.

High River

    On a pictured winter stroll, copse to river,

    you nurse the urn in the crook of your arm.

    The water's dimpled skin trembles at the brim,

    coils at the roots of willows.

    A promise kept -

    to die before you die -

    you cast your ashes to the high race of the river.

    Absorbed

    under the tips of jiggling catkins,

    under the perfect blue linen of the sky.

Haiku

her old haunt
the snowdrops
unchanged

a far view
trees then misty trees
then mist

nothing said
the stone axe
weighed in his palm

a blackbird's song
holding the hoe
above the weed

the ebb
of a swan's wingbeat
into river fog

Field And Sky

At the sallow's gap

we step through the hedge

and are nothing but field and sky.

Hares race, lurching

to a tussle,

their frenzy printed in the soil.

The kestrel soars -

pausing, head down,

to sew with the finest needle.

Equinox

    Fieldfares rattle from tree to tree northwards.

    One robin pitches

    its fierce songs

    into the silences of another.

    A small buzz

    hurtles from the world's core, a bumble bee

    in its wake.

Morning Walk

Your hat

snatched by the hedge

hangs on a thorn.

My hand bent on retrieval

wishes simply

to stroke your cheek,

as the chugging boat's

reflection

skims the bright water.

Bumble Bee

Crawling

among blackthorn stars,

the bumble bee is drunk.

Petals float

from her blunders.

Her wings

move in and out of humming.

On her body is the glory

of the sun's

wet shine.

Sunday

Threads of gossamer, shimmering

currents,

drift through the garden.

The cherry tree receives you,

stains you

with blossom, sunlit and shadowed pinks.

In the distance, the clouds are deepened

with a smudge

of grey, the loosening of rain.

Summer Rain

> The light is sunk here
>
> like a tin ladle.
>
> Beads captive on velvet
>
> bend the leaves of barley.
>
> The dust leaks
>
> a familiar fragrance.
>
> And your bare arms disclose
>
> how intricate
>
> skin can be, cool and wet.

Lullaby

    River stationed,

    the damselfly

    has stilled its wings,

    blue lace folded

    on a hunter's slenderness.

    Perch, slanted from their mouths,

    speak to the surface an

    occasional O.

    Lily pads are sunk and curled

    by the river's rub,

    papooses

    nodding in the waterlight.

Shady Trees

    Heat at midday

    dovetails to the earth.

    Our feet knock on baked clay.

    The cattle tread a slow mill.

    Their shady trees

    roll down.

    The haze of the field is scented

    with beanflowers.

    Swifts loop the willows and rise -

    gleams, shadows

    on the high air.

Night Storm

The wind surges

where the small apples ride

and the leaves are shingle.

Flash and ghost-flash

pin the sky to hard earth

and the sky rends.

In one strange

momentary day

the tree is brought to us

to be known afresh.

We stand as nothing

and are wedded to a blaze

of leafed and appled radiance.

This Hour

    A gold stitch in the west frays

    and the sky peels to crimson.

    Rooks flying aslant cry for the roost.

    The small pates of mayweed glow.

    We are not strangers this hour

    to how the world breathes fire.

    Our dog in hedgerow gloom

    turns his head to a whistle,

    lolling the pink flare of his tongue.

Wind Chill

An elusive numbness grazes the few leaves

flicking on the poplar,

worms between thorns into the wren's thicket,

brushes the ditch nimbly with the fox,

wavering, a quiver of rust.

Wood Mouse

      Little sack

      of hourglass sand,

      elderberry eyes,

      feathered by torchlight to a wild dash

      and sneeze-like spring —

      whisker to whip-long tail

      into the midwinter

      dark.

Midwinter Sun

The lime tree,

a sheen brushed into its twigs,

imagines an orb of silver.

The horse blows at the shadow's edge

and buckles into the light,

wisps on her belly striking pale flames

as she rolls.

The far oak,

poised on the rim with the bulging sun,

steadies the slow descent.

Haiku

nothing inside us
stops the rain drumming
inside us

the burn of far lights
all the darkness
listening

winter trees
the last apple saved
for the horse

voices
travelling with the sky
wild geese

collapsing bonfire
in the starry sweep
of the night

A Child Melts Into His Day

    Whiskers of barley stroke the light

    in the field.

    The butterflies touch stillness, flattened

    to stones, wingtips dashed

    with red.

    The stones rest in their small

    cups of earth.

    Faintly

    the air breathes, anointed, through leaf

    and blossom.

A Skip Down The Lane

    High mist

    holds the summit of a cloud

    in a perfect glassy dome.

    She guides him into the meadow.

    The bird snaking

    with pinched out wings slowly

    waves into the whiteness.

    He presses her hand. Fetches

    a word - Heron,

    she says - for the wonder.

    All day

    the clouds will skirt the world,

    arch in the blue.

The Nag's Head

She finds them,

the snug ring of women,

the one small boy who cranes and is lost.

Fires inch round her neck and wrists,

measuring her.

Lavender. Sprigs tied with lace. Her words

clack on a loom.

She peers, nods at him. Blue-eyed, she says.

Sky inside him.

She goes, the door clicks shut, their relief

skims over

like a bevy of geese.

George

I saw him, watching
as a small boy
watches, but I never
heard him. He never spoke.
He passes in silence through
my remembering. His wire
boned stride flustering
the geese. A sack live
with a ferret in his grip.
Home is a ditched
railway carriage, miles
from the railway.
He sits inside, the door open.
I see him. Stiff on
his chair with hands at rest.
A goose egg in his palm.

I Find You

> I find you
>
> on the top step of
>
> the dark stairwell
>
> and we lean at the window.
>
> Eye to the glass.
>
> Moths are dabbing at the doorlight.
>
> Such pale wings.
>
> The swifts are sooted out. Their night
>
> flutters like a scarf.
>
> Deep in the blackness
>
> there's a wind
>
> glowing the stars.

With Olly And Isaac In August

> We poke about
>
> in the shade of elder, the cobwebs peppered
>
> with dust.
>
> Earth scratched from a badger tunnel
>
> is heaped reddish-brown.
>
> At a hole
>
> dug for nightly visits
>
> our shadows come together.
>
> Intently
>
> we pierce with sticks the soft, yielding cake
>
> of badger dung.
>
> A bee knocks against us,
>
> untroubled.
>
> On my sleeve a dash of pollen.

Jewel

Hurt keeps you

a child. Will always keep you.

I stand at your side in

the paddock. A calm

hour. You do not flinch

or run wild. You fondle

the goat…gently

wring your sleeve from

his mouth…deep

inside the jewel of this moment

bend close

to his mischievous eye.

Dragonflies

Watch me, he says.

And he smears

blackberries on his face. Wounded.

Bleeding his Apache

blood. He staggers from the hedge.

Falls on his brother

who rolls and swears and picks up a clod.

And the dragonflies come down.

Settle on a hand, a knee,

an ankle. Nodding their heads. Sunlight

floating on their wings.

Far from the river. Come far

in the sun. Peaceably

over the dry fields.

Kindling

>Five and a pram clatter from the woods
>and turn for home.
>
>One boy pushes, the other steadies the load.
>Their mother
>will trudge to the world's end.
>
>The cousins clip
>ahead. Socks with a sting of white.
>Hands in a clasp
>
>an inch from their faces.
>And they lean together. Soft cheeks to
>the knuckles.
>
>Leaf sands leaf in the trees. Long shadows
>inhabit the lane.

Fetching The Boy

    Where's the boy? I call.

    He thunders on the stairs. Scrapes his boots

    pleasurably on the road.

    Under trees we crouch to the snowdrops. A faint

    trembling. The surprised splay

    of their petals.

    Now traipsing in the meadow he stops

    and looks up.

    Today

    the rooks are thrown ragged, the light pouring

    on the black of their feathers

    a shining oil.

Blue

You crouch over mucus

and blood fanning in the bowl.

Red is burning in your ribs.

Red is haunting the air.

You gasp, cry OOO as it comes.

In the lull you pad up the stairs

to what awaits you.

O let it be blue -

beyond the purr of our voices

and the owl calling into the night -

a soft, enfolding blue.

Days Later

    I'm the boy

    in the playground. Suddenly

    invisible. I'm speaking

    to myself. And I'm telling

    what's true. Telling

    of what's utterly gone.

    And I listen to myself

    and know.

    As the dog

    strangely

    on the night knew.

    As the dog told what was true,

    in the dark, inconsolable.

To Tip A Word

> She stands at my door.
>
> Shows a billycan, a packet
>
> of tea. Pale blue eyes. Oil
>
> in her frown. I ask her in.
>
> Reluctant, she dips to a stool.
>
> The rubbed grime of her coat
>
> folds in a dark
>
> lustre. I boil water,
>
> make a parcel of bread and cheese.
>
> She moistens her lips. Rocks
>
> as if to tip a word from
>
> the brim of herself. I wait
>
> suspended. Until,
>
> through the window,
>
> the last of the evening light
>
> is upon us.

Chestnut Loke

> Arcade gloom, leafy heights
> loosening the burrs.
>
> Chestnuts spill on hard dirt,
> silky shells
> with light in their bellies.
>
> Stooped
> I catch the Sunday shine of boots
> moving beside me.
>
> Together we'll set nuts
> close to the coals. Roll them hot
> in the palm.
>
> Savour the singed black, the sweet
> smoky pieces.

Sparrowhawk

Sparrows buzz for cover

and she comes

riding her tail to peer into the leaves.

She turns and

drives at the sky mirrored in our house

and rams the glass.

I smooth her undone

feathers,

rest her head on the crook of my finger.

And I wait in the wild light of the field

watching

for her eye to open.

Migrating Frogs

>What have I brought you?
>
>News heard in disbelief. Grief
>
>I've brought you.
>
>You sob. And when you speak
>
>I hear a child's
>
>voice. A long-ago voice
>
>flashed awake.
>
>And I see you. In the dark,
>
>in the rain. A lamp
>
>coming up the lane to meet you.
>
>He hoists you
>
>piggyback to take you home.
>
>And you ride
>
>over the frogs, light in their
>
>eyes, poised on their shadows.
>
>Migrating hundreds. On the ruts,
>
>in the rain. Steady,
>
>picking his way
>
>with care, he takes you home.

The Kiss

She comes in a dream.

She comes to retrieve

her final days,

the bruised frailty,

and set in their place

another time. I stand

before her in the scuffed light

of a station, the end of

a visit, her daughter

newly beside me.

She wears a summer dress.

Her goodbye

is a deft kiss. In the pool

of memory

it switches down

like a silver coin. I wake

from the dream to the first

hint of morning. Remember

the kiss, she says.

A Root Of Mint

> The scent rubbed from a leaf
>
> brings them.
>
> My grandparents
>
> poised in their trap. The pony
>
> reined to a stillness.
>
> Wait, I say.
>
> And curl this root with
>
> a crumble of earth,
>
> reach to the polished
>
> wheelguard, place it in the cup
>
> of my grandmother's hand,
>
> her pleasure
>
> tangible as wood or leather.
>
> And I step back.
>
> Seeing the pony quiver,
>
> hearing the click
>
> of my grandfather's tongue.

Only The Names

Names elude her. Even

that of her daughter

visiting daily.

The wind ruffles

her garden. The tulips redden

in their delicate shadows.

A story comes. She picks

a corner and sees it

unfold. Only the names

give her pause.

She bids her daughter goodbye,

then waits unsure.

Waits on memory's cuckoo

game. At the click

of the gate she finds her,

and calls her name.

To Douglas

    Arriving late in the day

    I join you

    at your window. You offer me

    the last of the light.

    Sparrows fly the soft

    smoke of the air. Their flock

    will haunt the laurel.

    You are still. A stillness

    embedded long ago

    in Sunday prayer.

    I've brought you this book, these lines

    from Keats.

    His step into oneness

    when he becomes

    like a floating spirit.

    You clasp your hands,

    ready to listen.

    Keats, you say. As if naming

    a friend.

I Walk Into The Weather

I walk into the weather. No news

of your coming. Unless this flood of joy

is news.

A dark fabric slides

down the sky. The path rattles, blinded.

In moments the light is falling in the trees,

the hail dizzied on

the ground.

I return weightless. And hear of your coming.

I imagine your plane in a high cruise,

a gleam of silver

catching someone's eye.

Caedmon

>Caedmon I heard in the barn.
>Not mumbling comfort in a cow's ear
>but singing.
>
>I was enthralled.
>Tiny fires were fanned in the dust.
>
>In a dream his song had begun to flutter
>inside him.
>One of those small deaths set it free, he said.
>
>Praise he sang.
>The mist was rising there and the world pristine.
>
>And that music searched us as we listened.
>Bitter rinds
>were peeled from our hearts.
>
>A strange turn, he said.
>Who dissolved me in such dark wonders?

If I Could

His wish. To walk

on the shore.

His clothes loose about him.

A familiar shore.

The wind strokes the sea

like a bell. Strokes it

to a murmur.

I'd raise him from his delirium.

The fish in the shallows

dart and bend their

silvers to the light.

And I'd bring him

to breathe

the sea's unmeasured air.

Saying Goodnight

His last night.

He's asleep, I said

and turned from the door.

I see him now. His face

in a drowse.

I sit at the fireside. A brow

of ash on the coals.

Bright flecks

in the soot. Lights on a hill.

He wakes but doesn't

know me. I press his hand.

His veins nudge

my fingertips. Rivulets in

a dark meadow.

I've come to say

Goodnight. I say it now.

Haiku

strolling

by apple trees

the roundness of joy

a stretch

picking blackberries

behind the spider

cloud shadow

the rose hips

dimmed

the same gesture

whoever enters

the midge cloud

misted sloes

the hedge sheltering

my father's grave

Foxes

Nights in January I hear the vixen and once see the dog fox. An early morning they appear from the hedge and rise up together and bat each other. There in the field they mate. Lowered under him she squirms to dab at his muzzle with her nose.

Later at an old hole in the bank I see earth freshly dug out.

A May evening I walk the narrow pathway between hedge and field. Swallows skim the barley. Ahead, the vixen stands under a low branch, cubs at her side suckling. She waits a little then ducks to her den. The cubs haltingly venture towards me. Four, red-brown, black paws, amber eyes. The boldest stretches a nose, touches and gladdens me.

Haymaking

Here is my grandfather at work on a fine morning. His scythe, freshened in the dew, swishes on the slope to the river. A swathe of grasses and dandelion. Minutes pass and he stops to cross the blade with a whetstone. Unhurriedly above the world the swifts are turning the hours.

I know it well. At the scent of what falls today the horse will whinny and tremble.

Teasels

    Summer, I sit in my friend's kitchen. How can I help? I ask. Cut down the thistles in the pasture, she says. But spare the teasels.

    She fondly opens her book of wildflowers and reads to me. Leaves form cups that fill with rainwater, petals are rosy purple.

    Outside I savour the heat. The lime in the field is tall and sudden, a rush from skirt to crown. I swing the sickle, the thistles fall in their patches. My palm melts the grime of the handle.

    September, she'll set a vase of teasels on the sill facing south.

I Wake As Crystal

    Slowly, slowly it sifts down, my illness. I wake as crystal. Water chalky from the pump has found its clarity. Everything I turn to comes inside. A knock and visitors appear and charm me. I wear the look on their faces. Together we lean on the pasture gate. Now I'm utterly replaced by a horse walking its rim of fire into chestnut shade.

The Early World

    I recall the early world. How firmly I was placed on
its sill. In the kitchen at the open window my mother,
or my grandmother perhaps, spoke in my ear.
I saw a swan raised in that moment out of nothing.
The willow bowed, the reeds quivered, and a
milk white amazement dawned on the river.

About the writer

Colin Oliver was born in 1946 in Norfolk, England. He recalls a swan on the River Tas as his earliest memory and says that all his life rivers and meadows have inhabited his imagination. Study at Goldsmiths' College, London, led him to work for many years in primary education. He is married to Carole, with children and grandchildren, and lives in Suffolk close to the River Stour.

Printed in June 2019
by Rotomail Italia S.p.A., Vignate (MI) - Italy